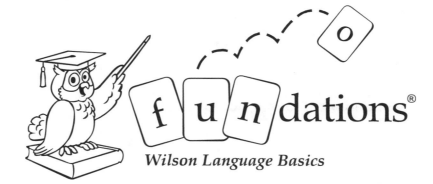

Wilson Language Basics

Student Notebook

Level 2

SECOND EDITION

Wilson Language Training Corporation

www.wilsonlanguage.com

www.fundations.com

Fundations® Student Notebook 2

Item # F2STNBK2

ISBN 978-1-56778-518-0

SECOND EDITION

PUBLISHED BY:

Wilson Language Training Corporation
47 Old Webster Road
Oxford, MA 01540
United States of America

(800) 899-8454

www.wilsonlanguage.com

Printed in the U.S.A.

November 2019

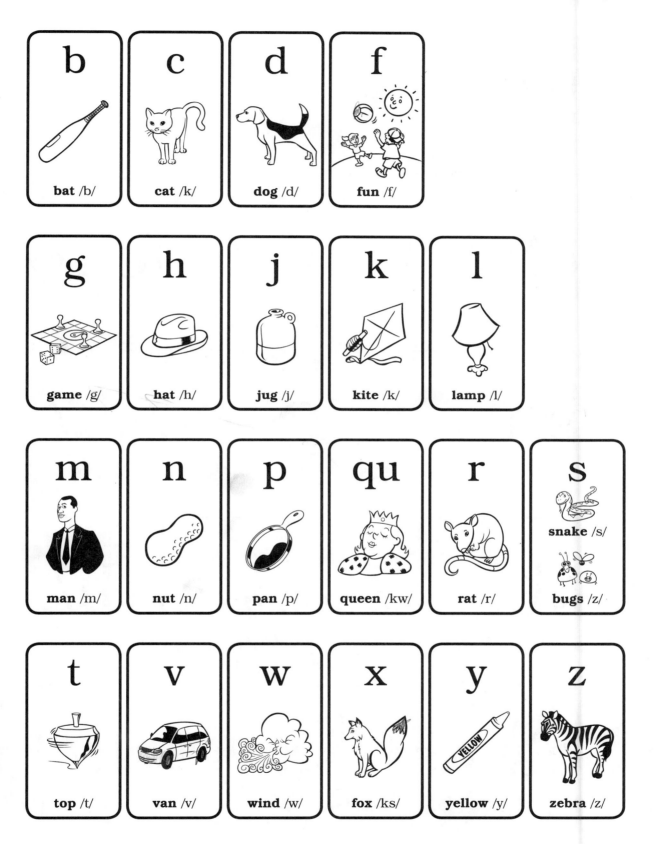

b	c	d	f
bat /b/	**cat** /k/	**dog** /d/	**fun** /f/

g	h	j	k	l
game /g/	**hat** /h/	**jug** /j/	**kite** /k/	**lamp** /l/

m	n	p	qu	r	s
man /m/	**nut** /n/	**pan** /p/	**queen** /kw/	**rat** /r/	**snake** /s/ **bugs** /z/

t	v	w	x	y	z
top /t/	**van** /v/	**wind** /w/	**fox** /ks/	**yellow** /y/	**zebra** /z/

Digraphs

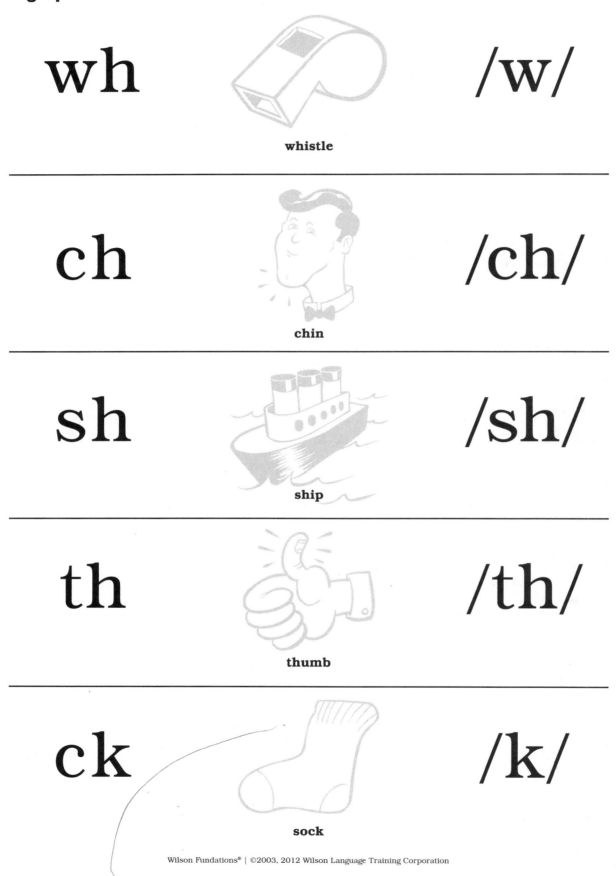

wh	whistle	/w/
ch	chin	/ch/
sh	ship	/sh/
th	thumb	/th/
ck	sock	/k/

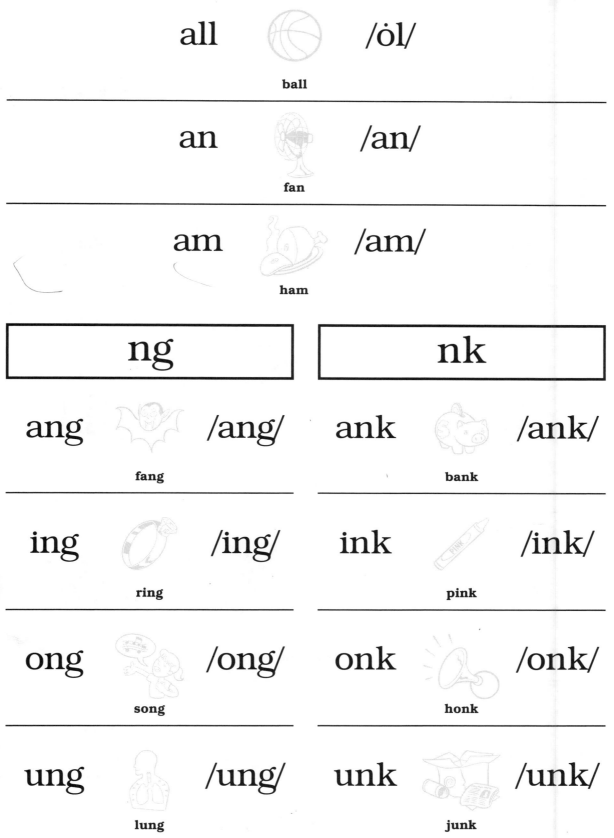

all /ȯl/

ball

an /an/

fan

am /am/

ham

ng	nk
ang /ang/	ank /ank/
fang	bank
ing /ing/	ink /ink/
ring	pink
ong /ong/	onk /onk/
song	honk
ung /ung/	unk /unk/
lung	junk

Short Vowels

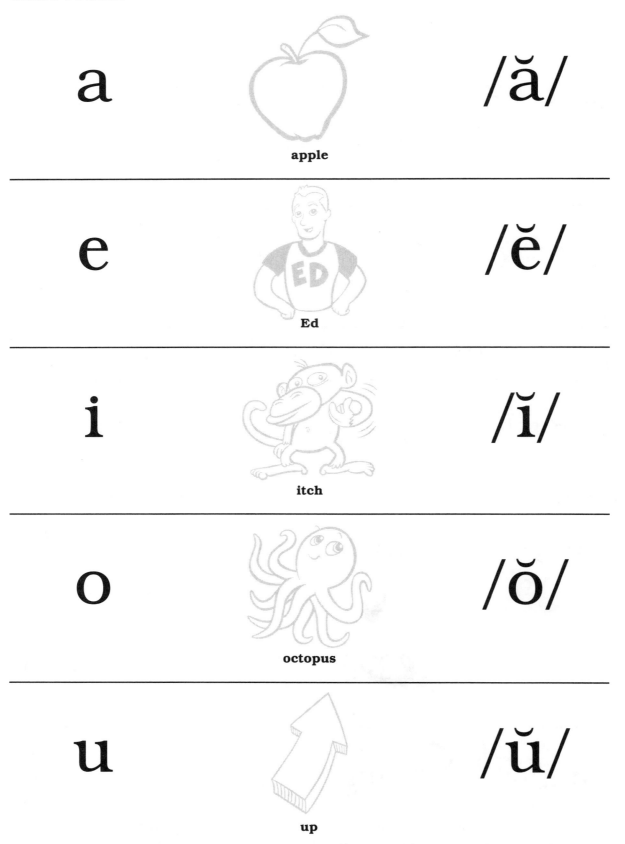

a	apple	/ă/
e	Ed	/ĕ/
i	itch	/ĭ/
o	octopus	/ŏ/
u	up	/ŭ/

Wilson Fundations® | ©2003, 2012 Wilson Language Training Corporation

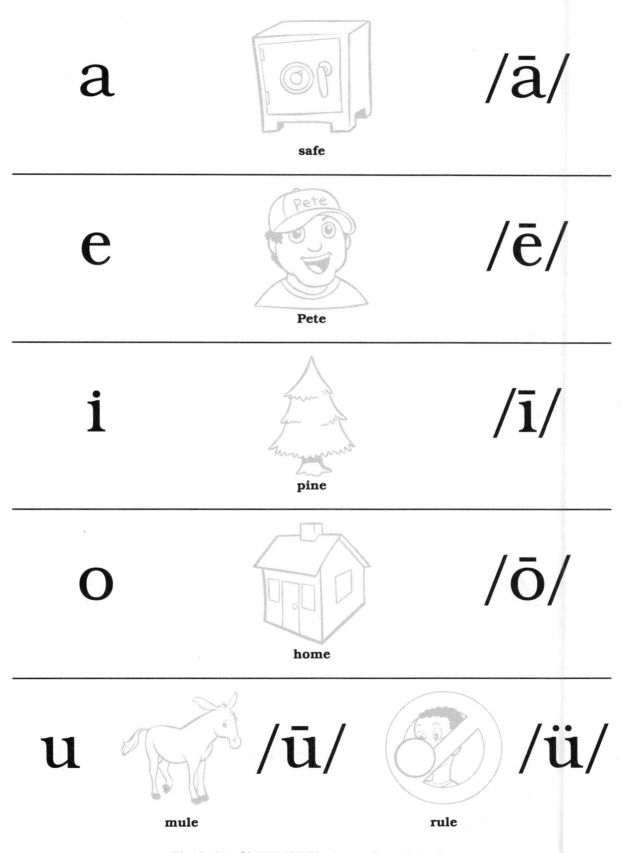

a

safe

/ā/

e

Pete

/ē/

i

pine

/ī/

o

home

/ō/

u

mule

/ū/

rule

/ü/

Vowels In Open Syllables

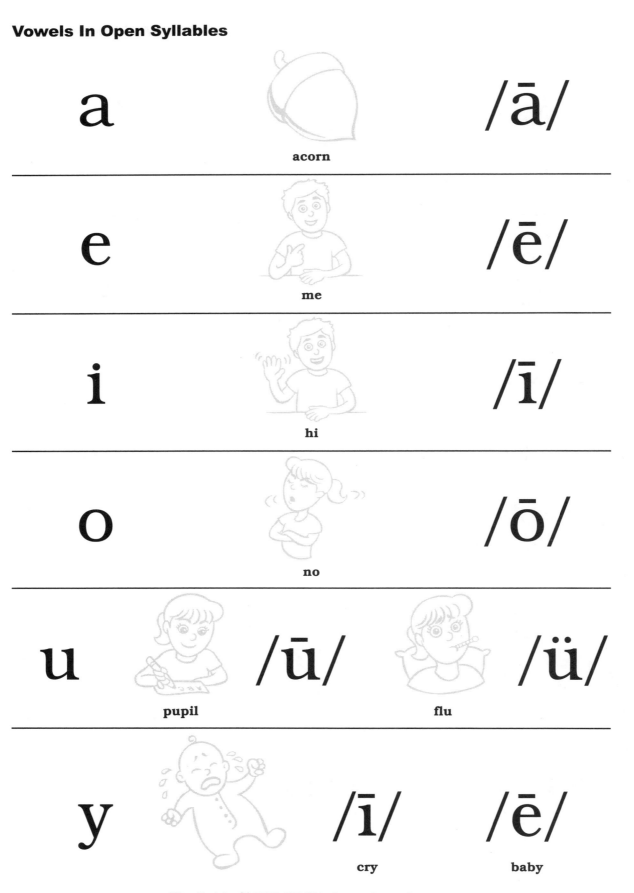

a	acorn	/ā/
e	me	/ē/
i	hi	/ī/
o	no	/ō/
u	pupil /ū/	flu /ü/
y	cry /ī/	baby /ē/

Vowels

Vowel	Closed Syllable	Vowel-Consonant-e Syllable	Vowel-Open Syllable

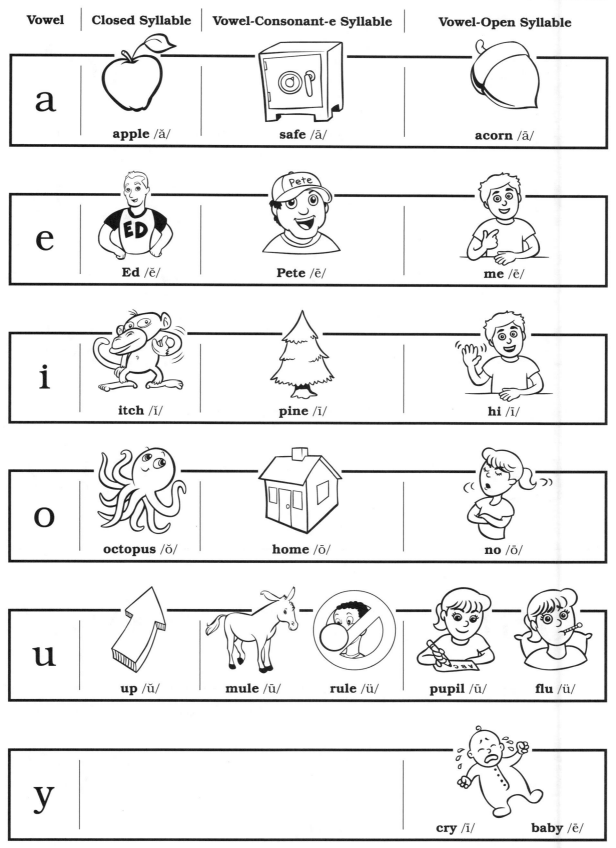

a — apple /ă/ — safe /ā/ — acorn /ā/

e — Ed /ĕ/ — Pete /ē/ — me /ē/

i — itch /ĭ/ — pine /ī/ — hi /ī/

o — octopus /ŏ/ — home /ō/ — no /ō/

u — up /ŭ/ — mule /ū/ — rule /ü/ — pupil /ū/ — flu /ü/

y — cry /ī/ — baby /ē/

Closed Syllable Exceptions

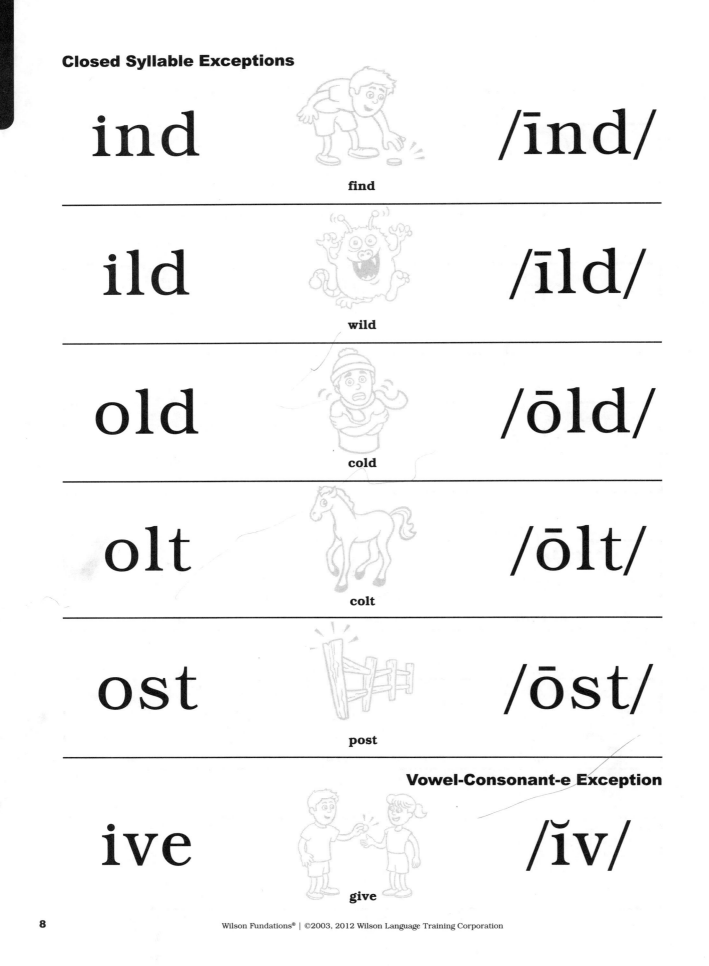

ind	find	/īnd/
ild	wild	/īld/
old	cold	/ōld/
olt	colt	/ōlt/
ost	post	/ōst/

Vowel-Consonant-e Exception

| ive | give | /ĭv/ |

R-Controlled Vowels

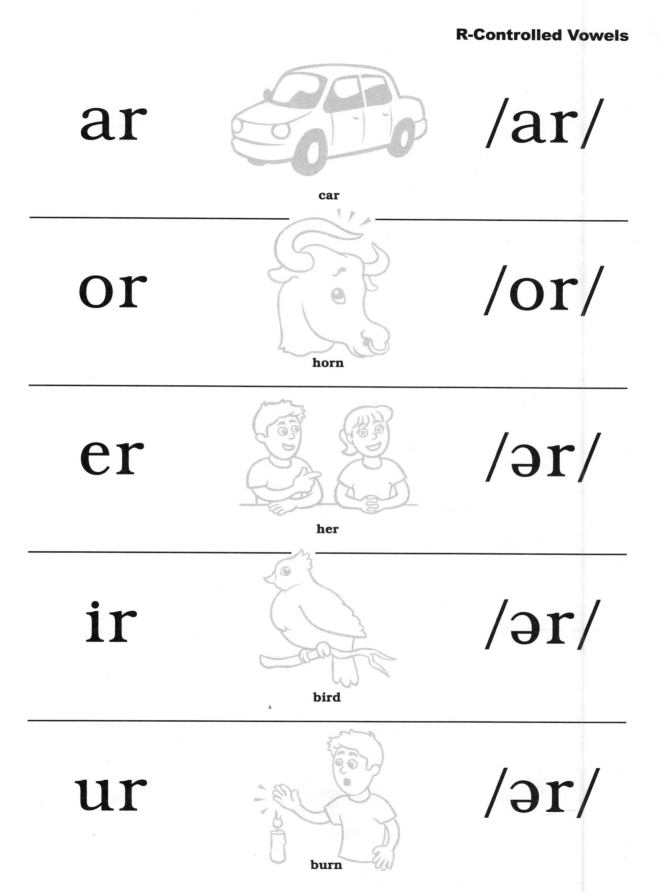

ar	car	/ar/
or	horn	/or/
er	her	/ər/
ir	bird	/ər/
ur	burn	/ər/

Vowel Teams

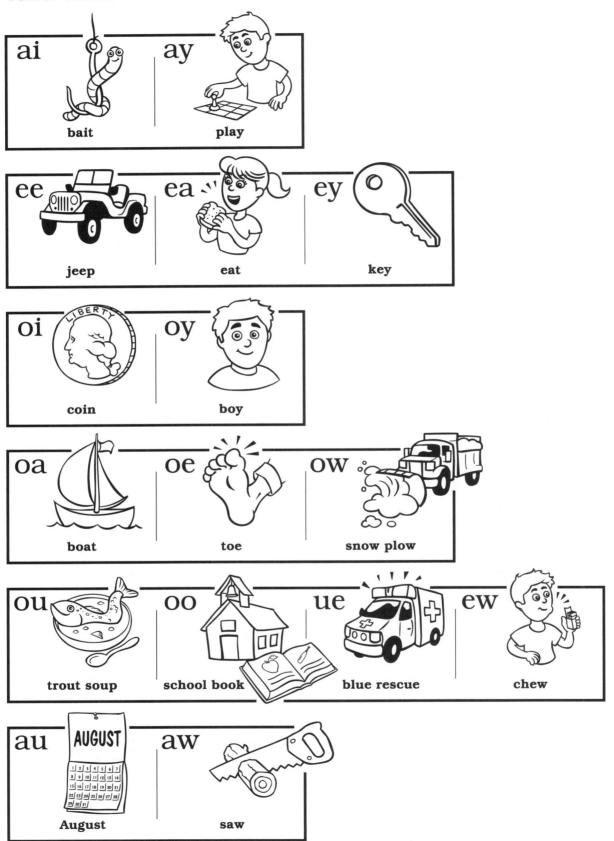

ai — bait

ay — play

ee — jeep

ea — eat

ey — key

oi — coin

oy — boy

oa — boat

oe — toe

ow — snow plow

ou — trout soup

oo — school book

ue — blue rescue

ew — chew

au — August

aw — saw

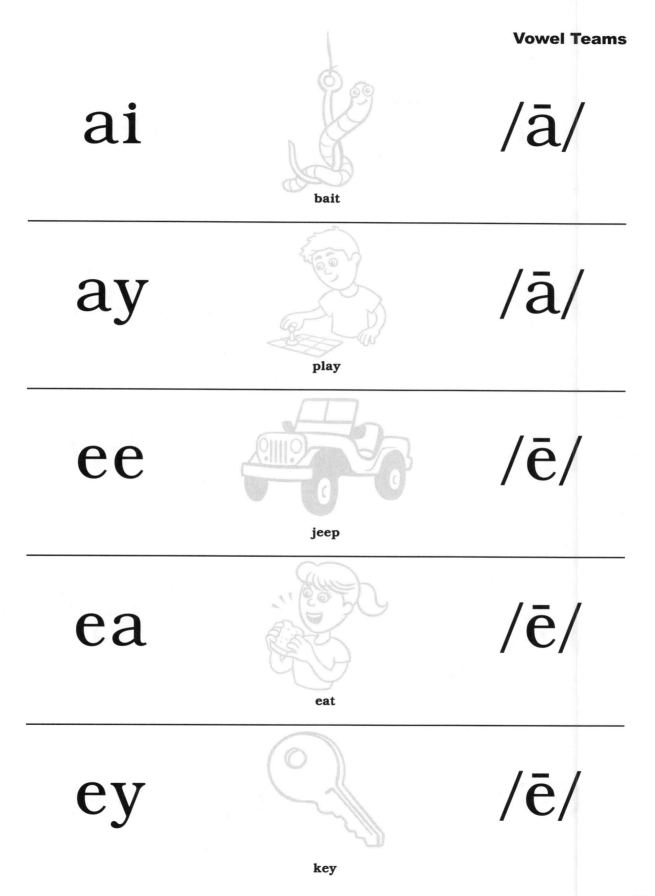

ai	bait	/ā/
ay	play	/ā/
ee	jeep	/ē/
ea	eat	/ē/
ey	key	/ē/

Vowel Teams

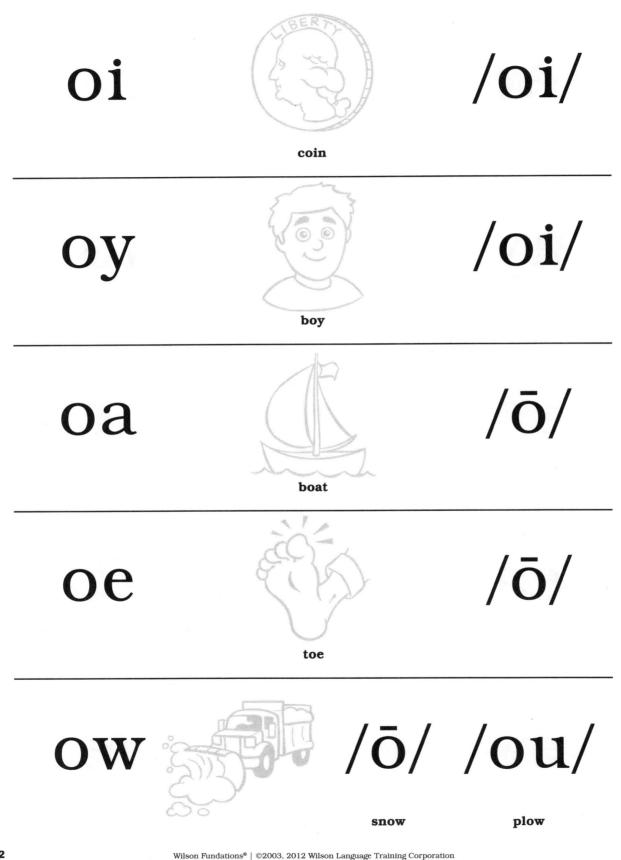

oi   coin   /oi/

oy   boy   /oi/

oa   boat   /ō/

oe   toe   /ō/

ow   /ō/ /ou/

snow   plow

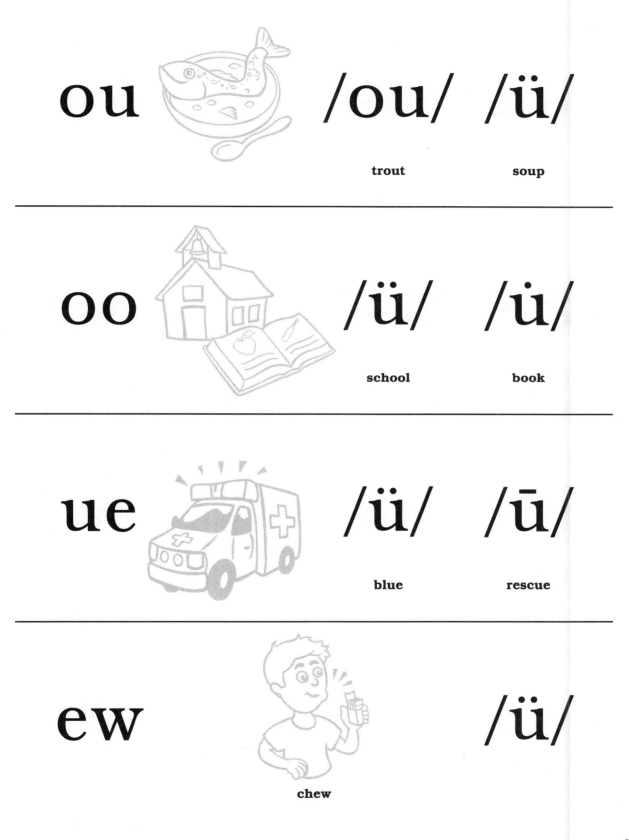

ou /ou/ /ü/

trout   soup

oo /ü/ /u̇/

school   book

ue /ü/ /ū/

blue   rescue

ew /ü/

chew

Vowel Teams

au

/ȯ/

August

---

aw

/ȯ/

saw

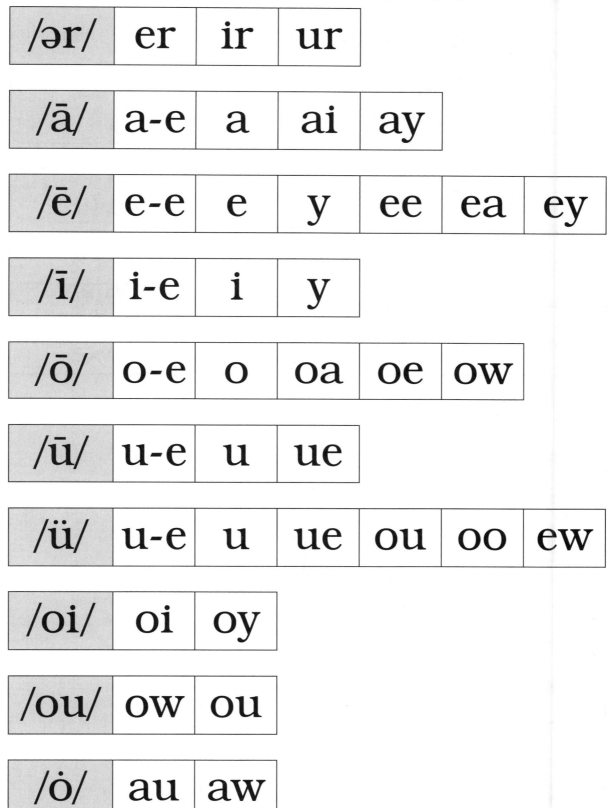

/ər/	er	ir	ur		
/ā/	a-e	a	ai	ay	
/ē/	e-e	e	y	ee	ea	ey
/ī/	i-e	i	y		
/ō/	o-e	o	oa	oe	ow
/ū/	u-e	u	ue		
/ü/	u-e	u	ue	ou	oo	ew
/oi/	oi	oy			
/ou/	ow	ou			
/ȯ/	au	aw			

What is a Syllable?

A syllable is a word or part of a word made by **one push of breath**.

A syllable must have a least **one vowel**.

closed syllable	$\dfrac{c\breve{a}t}{c}$	
v-e syllable	$\dfrac{c\bar{a}k\cancel{e}}{v\text{-}e}$	
open syllable	$\dfrac{m\bar{e}}{o}$	
r-controlled syllable	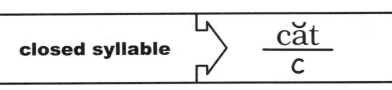	
"D" syllable	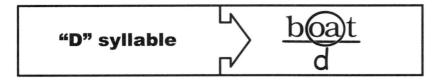	
-le syllable	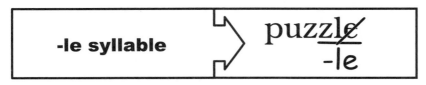	

Closed Syllables

1. This syllable can only have **one vowel**.

2. The vowel is followed by **one** or **more consonants** (closed in).

3. The vowel sound is **short**. To indicate the short sound, the vowel is marked with a breve (˘).

4. This syllable can be combined with other syllables to make **multisyllabic** words.

Exceptions: ind, ild, old, olt, ost words

The vowel is usually long even though it is in a closed syllable.

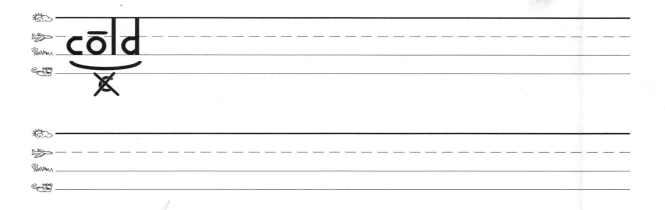

Vowel-Consonant-e Syllables

1. This syllable has a **vowel**, then a **consonant**, then an **e**.

2. The first vowel is **long**. To indicate the long sound, the vowel is marked with a macron (‾).

3. The **e** is silent.

4. This syllable can be combined with other syllables to make **multisyllabic** words.

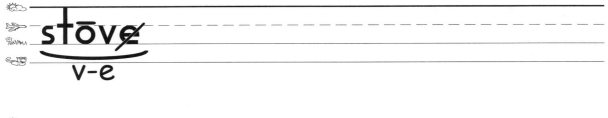

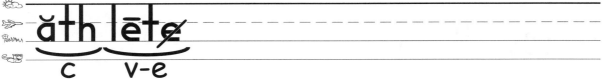

Exceptions: the letter **v**

Sometimes a word has a **vowel**, a **v**, then an **e**. The **e** may make the vowel long (**five**), or it may be there because English words do not end in a **v**. The vowel sound may still be short.

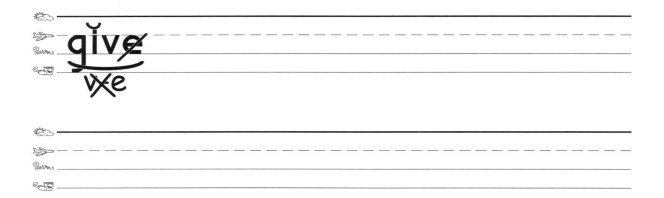

Open Syllables

1. This syllable has only **one vowel** which is the last letter in the syllable.

2. The vowel sound is **long**. To indicate the long sound, the vowel is marked with a macron (¯).

3. This syllable can be combined with other syllables to make **multisyllabic** words.

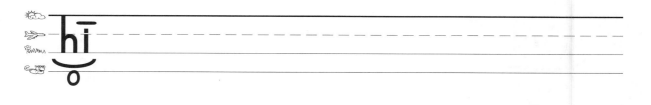

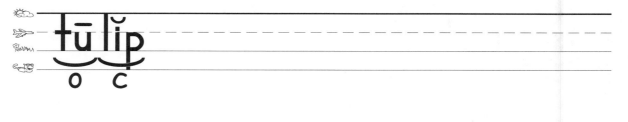

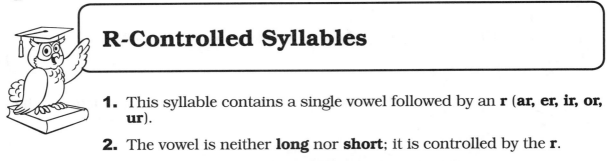

R-Controlled Syllables

1. This syllable contains a single vowel followed by an **r** (**ar, er, ir, or, ur**).

2. The vowel is neither **long** nor **short**; it is controlled by the **r**.

3. This syllable can be combined with other syllables to make **multisyllabic** words.

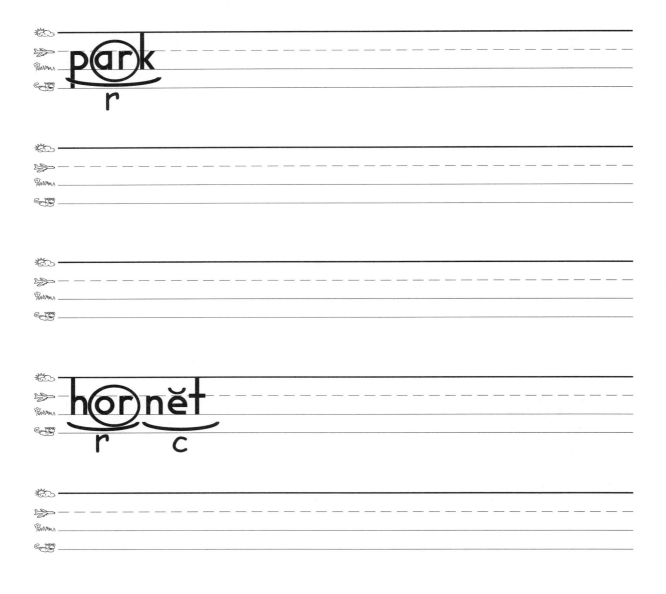

Vowel Digraph / Diphthong ("D" Syllables)

1. This syllable contains a **vowel digraph** or a **diphthong**. These are vowel teams.

Vowel Digraph:
Two vowels together that represent one sound (**ee**)

Diphthong:
A sound that begins with one vowel sound and glides into another (**oi**)

plain
d

ĕxplain
c   d

Consonant-le Syllables

1. This syllable has only three letters: a **consonant**, an **l**, and an **e**.

2. The **e** is silent. It is the vowel. Every syllable needs at least one vowel. The consonant and the l are sounded like a blend.

3. This syllable must be the last syllable in a **multisyllabic** word.

bŭb blĕ

c   -le

Wilson Fundations® | ©2003, 2012 Wilson Language Training Corporation

1 The Bonus Letter Rule for ff, ll, ss, and sometimes zz

At the end of a **one** syllable word, if the word ends in **one** vowel followed by an **f**, **l**, or **s**, you double that consonant.

ff   **ll**   **ss**

The letter **z** is also doubled in some words.

zz

The letter **a**, followed by a **double l**, does not have the expected short vowel sound.

all

Spelling Rules

SPELLING

2 Three Ways to Spell /k/ = c, k, ck

c cat /k/ | **k** kite /k/ | **ck** sock /k/

Use **c** at the beginning of most words.

<u>c</u>at

Use **c** when the /k/ sound is the first letter of a blend.

<u>c</u><u>r</u>ash

Use **c** in multi-syllabic words ending with **ic**.

picni<u>c</u>

Use **k** in glued sounds with **nk**.

p|ink|

Use **k** when the /k/ sound is the last letter of the blend.

mi<u>l</u><u>k</u>

Use **k** in vowel-consonant-e words.

bi<u>k</u>e

Use **ck** at the end of a one syllable word, right after the vowel.

so<u>ck</u>

Use **ck** in compound words.

humpba<u>ck</u>

Use **ck** after a short vowel with a consonant-le syllable.

ta<u>ck</u>le

3 The Baseword/Suffix Rules

Baseword

A **baseword** is a word that can stand alone as a word or have something added to it.

Suffix

A **suffix** is an ending that can be added to a baseword.

Plurals

A **plural** word is a word that means more than one thing. Nouns add **s** or **es** to make them plural.

Action Words

The **s** or **es** are also added to an **action** baseword or other verbs.

Most words add **s** to make them plural, or to show present action.

_____   _____

- - - - - - - - - - - - - - - - -   - - - - - - - - - - - - - - - - -

_____   _____

_____   _____

Words ending in **s**, **x**, **z**, **ch** and **sh** add **es**.

_____   _____

- - - - - - - - - - - - - - - - -   - - - - - - - - - - - - - - - - -

_____   _____

_____   _____

Vowel Suffixes

es

ing

ed /əd/

ed /d/

ed /t/

er

est

ish

able

en

ive

y

s

ful

ment

ness

less

ly

ty

SPELLING

Capitalization and Punctuation

 **Capital Letters**

A B C D E F
G H I J K L
M N O P Q R S
T U V W X Y Z

 Capitalization

- Beginning of sentence: <u>T</u>he dog is cute.
- People's names: <u>J</u>ohn and <u>M</u>aria are here.
- Specific names of places: <u>L</u>ong <u>P</u>ond, <u>W</u>isconsin
- Days of the week, months of the year: <u>F</u>riday, <u>J</u>une
- Beginning word in quote: Mr. Smith said, "<u>Y</u>es, I will go!"

 Punctuation

- Period (**.**): I am six years old.
- Question Mark (**?**): When will you visit?
- Exclamation Point (**!**): I love this class!

Other:

- Comma (**,**): September 1, 2012
- Quotes ("**" "**"): She asked, "How are you?"

A

angry
ape
archery
argue
astronaut
athlete
aunt
auto

B

baby
bait
bake
baseball
baseline
basic
be
beagle
beak
beast
beat
beaver
beef
beehive
beet
began
behave
behind
belly
below
beneath
beside
between
birch
bird
birth
blaze
bleed
blew
blister
blooming
blow

B

blown
blue
boat
boil
boiled
bone
book
boom
bow
boy
boy scout
braid
brain
brave
brawl
broil
broke
brook
brown
brute
buggy
bunny
burn
burp
by

C

cake
came
candy
cane
care
cartoon
case
cave
caveman
chain
chapter
charcoal
chase
cheap
cheek
chew
chilly
chimney
chimpanzee
chirp
choke
chose
chowder
church
churn
classy
claw
clay
close
cloud
cloudy
clover

Spelling Options

C	C	D	E
clown	creek	daddy	eat
coach	crook	dare	eject
coal	crouch	Dave	elbow
coast	croup	day	empty
coasting	crow	dear	enjoy
coat	crowd	deer	enjoyed
cockroach	crown	defend	entertain
coleslaw	crunchy	define	entertainment
complain	cry	delay	exhale
complained	cube	depend	explain
complete	cue	destroy	explained
concrete	Cupid	dew	explode
cone	curl	dirt	
confuse	curly	dirty	
consider	cursive	discount	
contain	curtsy	disturb	
continue		dizzy	
corner		doe	
costume		donate	
couch		donkey	
couches		down	
count		doze	
cow		drain	
cozy		draw	
cradle		drawn	
crane		dream	
crawl		drew	
crawling		drool	
crayon		drown	
craze		due	
crazy		Duke	
creak		duty	

Wilson Fundations® | ©2003, 2012 Wilson Language Training Corporation

F	G	H	I
faint	girl	handy	I
farmer	gloat	happy	igloo
fault	globe	hate	include
feast	glow	haul	indeed
feed	glue	haunt	inflate
fern	go	haunted	ivy
fifteen	goat	hawk	
fifty	good	hay	
fir	gown	haze	
first	grade	he	
flagpole	grain	heat	
flame	granny	her	
flea	grape	hi	
flirt	grapevine	ho	
flow	grave	hockey	
flowed	gravy	hoe	
flower	gray	hole	
flu	graze	holly	
fluffy	grew	holy	
flute	groan	home	
fly	ground	hooded	
foam	group	hook	
foolish	grow	hoop	
foot	grown	hope	
football	grumpy	hose	
foul		hotel	
found		hound	
frown		humid	
frowned		hurt	
froze			
fry			
fuse			

Spelling Options

J	K	L	M
Jake	Kate	lady	maid
Jane	keep	lake	mail
jeep	key	lane	main
jelly	kidney	lantern	male
jigsaw		late	mane
join		launch	marble
joint		launching	may
joke		laundry	maybe
jolly		law	maze
joy		lay	me
June		lazy	meat
		leaf	meet
		leash	mermaid
		load	mildew
		loaf	moist
		lobby	monster
		lobster	moon
		locate	motel
		loud	mow
		louder	muggy
		lousy	mule
		low	my
		lucky	
		Luke	
		lumpy	

N

name
nasty
native
navy
need
needle
new
no
noisy
noon
nose
note
now

O

oak
ouch
out
outgrew
outline
outside
outstanding
overdue
owl
own

P

paid
pail
pain
paint
painting
pale
pane
panther
pantry
Paul
pay
peacock
peanut
penny
perch
perfect
perfectly
perfume
Pete
pew
pewter
plain
plane
plaster
plate
playpen
plenty
plow
point
poke
pole
pony

P

pose
postpone
pouch
pound
pounding
pouting
powder
power
pray
predict
pretend
pro
program
prune
pry
puny
puppy
purple

M N O P Qu R S

Spelling Options

Qu	R	S	S
quake	raid	safe	showed
queen	railroad	sale	shower
	rain	save	shown
	rainbow	saw	shy
	raindrops	sawdust	silly
	raw	say	sir
	rawhide	scooping	sixteen
	ray	scooter	skirt
	read	scout	sky
	relax	scrape	slope
	remind	scrawny	sly
	repeat	screw	smooth
	rescue	seam	snake
	retire	seem	sneakers
	return	seesaw	snout
	returned	serve	snow
	road	shake	snowball
	roadblock	shampoo	snowed
	roast	shape	snowstorm
	robot	share	so
	rode	shave	soak
	rooster	shawl	soaked
	rope	she	soil
	rose	sheep	solo
	rotate	sheet	sound
	round	shipload	soup
	rowdy	shirt	south
	ruby	shook	sparkle
	rule	shoot	speak
	ruler	shout	speech
	runway	shouted	spider
		show	spoil

MNOPQuRS

S

spoke
spook
spooky
sprain
spray
sprawl
squeak
squirm
squirt
stampede
staple
state
stay
steam
stern
Steve
stew
sticky
stir
stone
stood
straw
stray
streak
street
sturdy
subway
sunrise
surf
surprise
survive
sweep
swirl

T

table
tadpole
taffy
tail
take
tale
tape
tea
teach
teacher
teacup
team
tee
teeth
temper
term
termite
these
thirsty
thirteen
thirty
those
throat
throne
throw
thrown
thunder
thunderstorm
Thursday
tidy
tinfoil
tiptoe

T

toad
toast
toaster
toe
tolerate
tomboy
took
tow
tower
toy
trade
train
tray
treat
trolley
trombone
trout
true
tube
tulip
tune
turbulent
turkey
turn
turned
turnips
turtle
turtles
twirl

U

ugly
understand
understood
unit
unsafe
use

TUVWXYZ

Spelling Options

V	W	Y
valley	waist	yawn
value	wait	yawned
vase	waited	you
verb	wave	youth
volume	way	
vote	we	
	weak	
	week	
	weep	
	whale	
	wheel	
	whine	
	whirl	
	why	
	window	
	windy	
	wood	

Aa

Aa Aa A

Aa

Bb

Vocabulary

Bb

Bb

Bb

Bb

Bb

Bb

Vocabulary

Cc

Cc

Cc

Vocabulary

Cc

Cc

Cc

Vocabulary

Cc

Dd

Dd

Vocabulary

Dd

Dd

Dd

Vocabulary

Dd   Dd D Dd   D

Dd

Dd

Dd

Ee

Ff

Tuesday February 2
(Gym)

Vocabulary

Ff
law   Karim

letters   3

vowels   1

Ff
Sounds 2   Consonants 2

Dot break the law

Ff

023

Ff

Ff

Ff

Wilson Fundations® | ©2003, 2012 Wilson Language Training Corporation

Vocabulary

F f

G g

G g

Gg

Gg

Hh

Vocabulary

Hh

Hh

Hh

Jj

Jj

Kk

GHIJKL

Vocabulary

Kk

Ll

Mm

Mm

Nn

Nn

MNOPQuRS

Vocabulary

Nn

Oo

Oo

Wilson Fundations® | ©2003, 2012 Wilson Language Training Corporation

MNOPQuRS

Pp

Pp

Qu qu

Vocabulary

Qu qu

Rr

Rr

Rr

Rr

Rr

MNOPQuRS

Vocabulary

Ss

Ss

Ss

Ss

Ss

Ss

MNOPQuRS

Vocabulary

S s

S s

S s

Wilson Fundations® | ©2003, 2012 Wilson Language Training Corporation

S s

S s

S s

MNOPQuRS

Vocabulary

T t

T t

T t

TUVWXYZ

Tt

Tt

Tt

TUVWXYZ

Vocabulary

T t

V v

V v

Ww

Vocabulary

Wilson Fundations® | ©2003, 2012 Wilson Language Training Corporation

Aa	a	another
	about	any
	also	are
L1	and	as

Bb	be	by
	been	
	being	
L1	between	

Aa

Bb

Aa

Bb

Aa

Bb

Aa

Bb

Aa

Bb

Aa

Bb

Aa

Bb

Aa

Bb

Trick Words

Cc	called
	come
L1	could

Dd	day
	do
	does
L1	down

Cc

Dd

Cc

Dd

Cc

Dd

Cc

Dd

Cc

Dd

Cc

Dd

Cc

Dd

Cc

Dd

Trick Words

Ee	each
L1	

Ff	first
	for
	friend
L1	from

Ee

Ff

Ee

Ff

Ee

Ff

Ee

Ff

Ee

Ff

Ee

Ff

Ee

Ff

Ee

Ff

Trick Words

Gg	good
L1	

Gg

Gg

Hh	has	here
	have	his
	he	how
L1	her	

Hh

Hh

Hh

Ii	I
	into
	is
L1	

Ii

Jj	
L1	

Jj

Jj

Kk	
L1	

Kk

Kk

Ll	little
	look
L1	

Ll

Ll

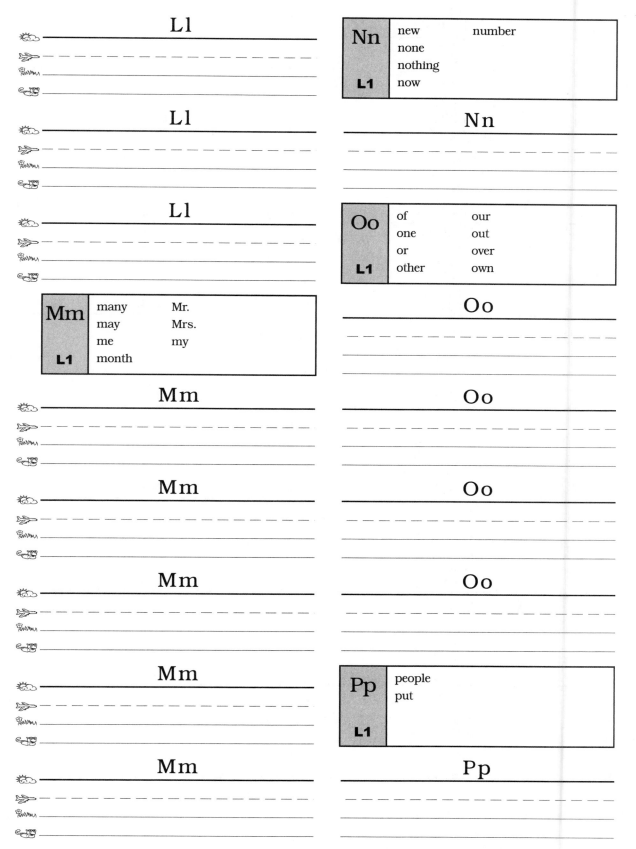

Ll

Ll

Ll

Mm	many	Mr.
	may	Mrs.
	me	my
L1	month	

Mm

Mm

Mm

Mm

Mm

Nn	new	number
	none	
	nothing	
L1	now	

Nn

Oo	of	our
	one	out
	or	over
L1	other	own

Oo

Oo

Oo

Oo

Pp	people
	put
L1	

Pp

M N O P Qu R S

Trick Words

Pp

Pp

Pp

Pp

Pp

Rr
L1

Rr

Rr

Rr

Rr

Rr

Ss	said	she
	say	should
	says	some
L1	see	

Ss

Ss

Ss

Ss

Ss

Ss

Ss	Tt
Ss	Tt
Ss	Tt
Ss	Tt
Ss	Tt

Tt	the	to
	their	too
	there	try
L1	they	two

Uu	
L1	

Tt	Uu
Tt	Uu
Tt	Uu

TUVWXYZ

Trick Words

Vv	very
L1	

Vv

Vv

Vv

Vv

Ww	want	were	who	would
	was	what	why	write
	water	when	word	
L1	we	where	work	

Ww

Ww

Ww

Ww

Ww

Ww

Yy	you
	your
L1	

Yy

Yy

NOTES

NOTES

Sky Line Letters

t b f l h k

Plane Line Letters

n m i u r p j

Plane Line Round Letters   Special e

c o a g d s q   e

Plane Line Slide Letters

v w y x z